Short Tales Told (Dark Stories of Love & Lust)

Jo Ann Atcheson Gray, Jo Jo Gray, Anna Elizabeth, Sasha Joy

Contents

Short Tales Told (Dark Stories of Love & Lust)

Chapter 1: Sacred Choice (Between Good & Evil) By Anna Elizabeth

Decisions...Choices... It's all a part of life. I'm named Terri Tessa Ann, but everyone calls me Terri. I'm just a simple girl who loves books, especially the old ones. I currently work in the local library in the heart of South Florida. I love my job! I'm thirty-three years of age and of African American decent. I'm petite with brown eyes and thick black curly hair.

I reside in my own apartment as my parents still live in the lower part of South Florida. My commute to their house is only thirty-five minutes. I keep a routine, weekly check on them. My Mother and Father raised me to be a respectable woman with good values and virtue. They showered me with much love and kindness.

This is where I'd like to tell my story...

One morning while arranging some dusty old books on the shelf at the library, I received a phone call from my parent's closest neighbor. This neighbor commenced by telling me that my parents had been in an accident early this morning. I knew they had taken a trip to the beach in Gulf Shores which was their regular vacation spot, and I suppose they were traveling home when another automobile hit them head on, killing them both instantly.

I was saddened and very broken hearted at this tragic news. After getting my wits about me, I drove to the local hospital and went straight to the morgue where my parents' bodies were kept. It was the hardest thing I think I had ever had to do. After identifying the bodies of my deceased parents, I headed to their home, my place of raising.

Looking around at my Mother's spotless abode, memories flooded through my mind of my childhood. All the love these two individuals showed me over the years. I must admit, I had the most awesome parents! My Father always surprised me with random trinkets after he would return home from work. My Mother would bake the best chocolate chip cookies along with a big glass of milk on most nights before going to bed. She always made me say my prayers before falling to sleep. She was an amazing, spiritual woman.

As days passed and their funeral was behind me, I knew I needed to sell the old house they lived in. There wasn't any way I could afford to keep it up. After a few weeks of advertising it, it finally sold.

The week before the new residents were to move in, I was cleaning out the small basement. I had already arranged for my parents' things to be stored in a storage facility until I could consider what I should sell and what I needed to keep. As I was rambling through some old, dusty filing cabinets, I found a stack of papers in the bottom drawer. These documents seemed important, so, I began looking them over.

I came across my birth certificate attached to a thick pile of paperwork. On my certificate was my given name along with a last name that I did not recognize. Also, on this paper was a different name for my Mother and Father. Flipping through the other stack of papers, I noticed it also had my name on it but with my corrected last name. It appeared to be my adoption papers. By the dates written on this birth certificate and these adoption papers, I was obviously adopted minutes after my actual birth, and it stated I was born in a local hospital in the state of Louisiana. New Orleans, to be exact.

I was dumbfounded, speechless. My parents never told me about this! Apparently, my birth parents were from New Orleans, and I was born there! So many questions swirled through my brain! My entire life here in South Florida was just a whole lie! No doubt I loved my parents, but they should've told me where I really came from!

After closing on the old house, I handed the keys to the new residents and left my place of raising. Dwelling in my apartment, my mind pondered about who I really was and where I actually came from. After searching for an address to the hospital that I was supposed to be born in, I prepared my luggage, booked my hotel, and planned my flight to New Orleans. I needed to know more about myself and where I was from, and who my actual birth parents were.

Catching a cab outside of the airport in New Orleans, I made my way to the famous French Quarter to my hotel. It was a beautiful residence, and many people were coming and going on the cobblestone streets. I felt at home at once. All the lovely buildings and artful people, it was amazing!

My room was cozy and nice. The queen size bed was very comfortable. After tossing my bags to the floor, I leaped onto the large bed and relaxed. Smiling a sad smile, I knew this place felt like 'home'.

The next morning, I dressed and headed to the free breakfast buffet downstairs. The bagels were delicious in this place! The coffee wasn't so great, but it was still caffeinated. After eating, I mentally prepared myself to venture to the local hospital in the city of New Orleans. I wanted answers to who my mother was and why she gave me away.

The hospital wasn't fancy or anything, it was dreary for the most part. I never liked places like this with all the 'sick' people in them. It made me shiver. At the information desk, I explained to the lady in the chair how I was adopted and needed to learn more about my birth mother. Chewing her gum, she said "Hold on, I will check on this for you."

When she returned to the desk in front of me, she was holding a small file of papers. Handing me the file she stated, "Those can't leave this hospital, but you're more than welcome to have a seat while you look them over."

After seating myself in a hard chair in the waiting area, I began looking through these papers. I discovered that my real mother was deceased, and she had died shortly after my birth. Apparently, my adopted parents were in this place the night I was born. It was arranged for them to take me that night. My real mother had placed me for adoption months before I was born, but why?

It showed in these records that she named me moments before her death, stating that I had to have the family name. It told of my grandmother, which her name was Tessa Terri Anne. Her signature was on every document in this file. Searching further, I found an address to where my grandmother lived. It was in the heart of the French Quarter.

Giving the file back to the gum chewing lady at the desk, I decided to go to this address and seek answers from my grandmother.

The address led to Royal Street to a little run-down store. This place was obviously a little voodoo shop. I had never been to a shop like this, so I was becoming slightly nervous. Getting the nerve to walk inside, I took a deep breath and thought to myself, 'It's now or never, Terri. You must get some answers.'

Inside was dark and depressing with herbal plants on shelves and trinkets of weird objects hanging from the ceiling. In the background, I heard some music playing softly as I approached the front counter made of glass. In this cabinet was strange items like incense, tarot cards, and jewels. I saw some shrunken heads decorated with lace and vines. It was quite 'creepy'.

Ringing the bell that was neatly resting on the edge of the counter, I waited for someone to assist me. Stepping out from the beaded curtains behind the counter was a lady of much age, dressed in a hobo style attire wearing many bracelets and a turquoise necklace. She had a turbine of pink silk nicely draped around her head and pearl earrings hanging from her ears. She was a lovely, dark-skinned woman.

Smiling, this lady asked if she could help me find anything. Clearing my throat, I explained to her who I was and who I was looking for. This beautiful lady began laughing and reached for hand patting it. Pulling me to side of the counter, she said, "Come on in child, I've been expecting you to come."

She led me through the beaded curtains to a room with nice, faded couches and several lit candles. Offering me some hot tea with lemon slices in it, she gestured for me to sit down. Placing herself across the little coffee table, she asked me, "So, my pretty lady, what took you so long to find me?"

After explaining to her in detail, I conversed with this mysterious lady for a long while. Discovering that she was my blood relative, my grandmother. My mother was her only child, and she left this world having me at the age of twenty-seven. My mother's real name was Anna Terri, and I looked a lot like her. My grandmother told me to call her Tessa while she began showing me photos of my mother and my father. They seemed so happy in the photographs.

"Well, what exactly happened to them? Please tell me!"

"My darling child, I will explain everything to you, but you must trust me with what I'm about to say to you."

"Of course, I will. Just tell me."

"Get comfortable while I put on some more tea and make us some beignets." Tessa stated as she left the little room.

When she returned, she had a large silver platter with beignets and cups of hot tea and lemons sliced next to them. Placing them on the coffee table she seated herself next to me and began speaking...

"Terri, your mother was a beautiful, creole woman with many gifts and talents. She was about to waste these 'gifts' on a man who wasn't good enough for her, which was your birth father. His name was Eric, and I despised him! He was a drifter and no good man who wanted to waste your mother's finances and carry her away from here. I could not allow such! Anna Terri was blinded by this and claimed she loved him, but I knew it was all fake love. So, I took care of him in my own way and never again heard from him.

You see, child, I have many talents of my own. It runs in our bloodline. Everyone in this French Quarter knows me as the local healer or the voodoo priestess. We descend from 'creole' blood. You, my child, are fully a creole descendant. These 'gifts' are in your blood. We come from a long line of voodoo queens and witches."

"Excuse me, I'm considered to be a witch or something?!"

"Be quiet, girl and let me finish telling you who you really are!"

Taking a sip of my warm tea, I listened as Tessa continued her tale..

"Your mother was an exceptional witch with many talents, yet she never wanted to practice these things. She tried avoiding who she really was, and it led to her death.

It started several centuries ago when one of our descendants made a pact with an evil being, and a 'curse' was placed on the women of our generations. Not really sure what caused this curse, but it has been passed to each of the females in our bloodline ever since. It's simply a curse that makes us decide whether we want to be a witch or practice voodoo. If there isn't a choice made when the 'curse' arrives, it will claim one's life instead. There is no running away from it once it catches up to you.

Anna Terri did not listen to me, and it overtook her the night you were born. She loved you but knew you would face these same choices. She tried to save you from this curse by placing you up for adoption and letting another family raise you far away from here. It did not work because you are here now!

It's a choice between Good & Evil, child! You must decide and soon! A witch or a Voodoo Priestess! It's already dwelling in your blood; I can feel it!"

"Wow, this is crazy! I think I understand, but it seems so unreal! I always knew I seemed different, but I had no idea I was this much different! Growing up, I would stare at candles, and they would light up. I just thought I was imagining such things. When I get angry or sad toward the other kids at school, they fall and get hurt. I never knew I was the one hurting them when I was angry. The thoughts would linger for days, but I would forget about it and try to remain normal. I never told my parents about it, yet I knew there was something strange about me. So, this is why I believe everything you are telling, Miss Tessa."

"Tessa, child, call me Tessa." She stated boldly with a smile.

"Understand, child, this curse can be different for each of us. One can never really know when it will overtake you, so, be ready and aware. When it comes, you will know! That's when you must make the choice! Good or evil! A witch or a voodoo priestess! Sometimes the choice is made for you, child. It's based on your gifts that you possess.

Now, go gather your things from the hotel and come back here! You will remain with me until this is passed, child. I have plenty of room. You will be safe and cared for here. Like I said, I have been waiting for you to come!"

After several weeks of being in the French Quarter with Tessa, I decided it best to relocate. So, I went back to Florida and packed all my belongings, sold my parents furniture and such, and returned to New Orleans. A fresh start, new job in the French Quarter Library, and a new way of life with my grandmother.

She taught me many things and many gifts that I was never aware that I possessed. I was learning so much about my ancestry and who I was meant to be.

Tessa was a voodoo priestess, yet she loved everyone. Her only flaw to me was when she would do a ritual for some stranger that involved hurting another individual. She would explain to me that sometimes it's not our business to ask questions, but to only accept the money and do what is asked of us. Then forget the experience and carry on.

"Just because one chooses evil doesn't mean I'm evil inside, child." Tessa would always assure me of this!

All my grandmother's practices made me realize I could never purposely harm someone for money! I did not want to do these 'evil' gestures! She would remind me on a daily basis that I had to choose a side. Whether I wanted to be good or not!

After several months of staying with Tessa, I began to practice herbal healing and different herbal spells that Tessa taught me. The spells came from my birth mother's journals. Tessa gave me these books after a week of being here and I feel I'm where I'm supposed to be, home.

One early, fall day, I was headed to the library when I stopped at the little coffee shop that just opened a few days back. I wanted to give this coffee shop a try. To make a long, boring story short, I met a man named Jonathan. I fell in love at first sight. He was slightly older than me, but his gray hair was so gorgeous with his eyeglasses resting on the tip of his nose. He was the owner of the little coffee shop and was new to the French Quarter. He moved here from Chicago after his wife passed away with cancer. He needed a fresh start and new surroundings.

Tessa did not like this courtship that I began having with Jonathan, but she never interfered. She would only tell me to be careful and don't get hurt by this man.

We fell in love and was becoming 'serious' when this 'curse' appeared to me. It was the fall of the next year when I felt these feelings of eagerness to practice my spells more and more. Of course, I told Jonathan about my ancestry and this curse that runs in my veins, yet he did not seem afraid.

One late evening, I expressed to my grandmother what I was feeling...

"Sit down, child, I want to tell you something." Tessa said. "I want to explain again to you the seriousness of your choice. Your mother, like I said, tried to run away from this curse, this choice. It ended her life! She chose to die rather than accept the curse. I do not want to watch you make the same mistake, child. This man that you are falling in love with will persuade you to leave and it won't be good for you! You have to let him go, child. You cannot live normally! Please, do not make the same fate as your mother did!"

"Jonathan is different, Tessa, he will understand. Besides, I've already told him about my curse and who I am. He's okay with it! He accepts me for who I am, and he loves me! He knows I must choose between good and evil, a witch or a voodoo priestess, and it fascinates him to know I'm gifted. Besides, I am fully aware that this 'curse' is upon me now. I've been feeling it for days."

"Well, just be cautious, child. I love you too much to see you follow in your mother's footsteps! Since those feelings have surfaced, it won't be long now, child. The next full moon will more than likely be the time to choose."

After Tessa left my bedroom, I decided to get some rest before going to work at the library in the morning. I had a planned dinner date with Jonathan that evening. I feltlike he was going to 'purpose' marriage at this dinner, so, I was anxious and excited! I did not tell my grandmother about my suspicions, because I knew she would panic at the thought of such. Trying to fade into a restful slumber, I heard the bell ring at the shop's front entrance. I figured it was someone seeking my grandmother's assistance again, so, I closed my eyes and slept.

That next evening, the moon was rising. It was going to be a lovely full moon kind of night. Of course, I was nervous at the thought of making such a choice, but I felt it was close at hand. I just needed to get through my dinner date with Jonathan and return home so my grandmother could be with me when I make the decision of good or evil.

When I arrived at the restaurant to meet Jonathan, he was not there. I waited for a few hours, and he still did not show. Deciding it best to head home before this 'curse' arose, I left the restaurant. My mind was swirling as to why Jonathan did not come. It wasn't like him to stand me up.

Tessa was sitting in the little parlor on one of the faded couches when I arrived home. Candles were lit all around the room. She gestured for me to have a seat next to her as she waved an incense stick smelling of fresh lavender around my face. She spoke, "Child, this is for your peace of mind and to help you be relaxed. It's only lavender. I'm not placing anything on you. Now, let's hear your choice."

Swallowing hard, I spoke in a whisper, "I do not want to harm anyone, so, I suppose I choose the way of a witch, Tessa."

My grandmother began laughing and assured me that it was over, and the choice was made. She explained that everything was okay now and that I could practice my 'gifts' and carry on with my life.

"So, that was it? No, craziness?" I asked, confused.

"Of course, child, that was it! What was you expecting? Fireworks or something?" Tessa replied with a smile.

"Well, I do feel different, yet I still feel the same."

"It's because the 'gift' is fully upon you now, child. Use it wisely!"

"I will, Tessa." I responded. "I'm just a little concerned about Jonathan. He did not show up for our dinner date tonight."

"No worries, child. He's right where he needs to be. Now, go on to the little coffee shop and you can find him there."

My mind pondered what Tessa had just told me as I left and headed to the coffee shop in search of Jonathan. Did my grandmother play a part in Jonathan's disappearance tonight? I guess it will forever be a mystery, yet I know deep inside she was involved. I knew she did not want me to mess up the same way my birth mother did. Funny thing was I never had any intentions on running from this curse. It was a responsibility I had to see through. I guess my grandmother was just being cautious.

When I got to the little coffee shop, the front light was on, and the door was unlocked. I found Jonathan behind the counter reading a book. He looked up at me and asked, "Where have you been, darling? I've been waiting on you all day!"

That's when I realized that Tessa had been involved in the night's happenings.

The next morning, I awoke and sitting on my windowsill was a beautiful owl of tan, white feathers. It looked at me and flew over to my bed, resting itself comfortably. I wasn't afraid of it. I felt like it was here to help me or something. Tessa explained later that day that this owl was my spiritual protector, and it would always be with me. She told me that all the witches in our creole bloodline possess some kind of spiritual animal. Apparently, mine is an owl.

That same day, I noticed that a dark, gray streak was in my hair. I panicked at first, but Tessa assured me it was normal. She told me of how my mother had the same gray streak in her hair as well as a black cat as her spiritual animal. She explained to me how Anna Terri would always run the black cat away, yet it always seemed to return to her.

Several days flew by as my 'gifts' felt stronger, more intense. I was becoming quite happy with who I was. That same night in the coffee shop, Jonathan asked for my hand in marriage, I said yes! After telling my grandmother about it, she was thrilled. She accepted Jonathan since I did not run from the curse.

After a simple, small wedding, I moved in with Jonathan in his apartment above the coffee shop. It was amazing! I was very happy being Jonathan's wife. He accepted me for who I was, witchy stuff and all. I think he was cautious of Tessa, but he never expressed it.

Some months later, Tessa finally confessed to me that she had placed a small 'charm' on Jonathan the night before so that he could not leave his coffee shop until I came to see him. I was angry at first, but I knew she couldn't harm him. She loved me too much to do such as that!

My life seemed to be going wonderfully. After a year of marriage, I discovered I was with child. Seven months in this pregnancy, I learned I was having a girl. My emotions were all mixed up. I was thrilled yet I was worried. I knew my daughter would have to face the same choice one day, good or evil, witch or voodoo priestess. I could only believe her choice would be for good and not evil. I was determined to teach her my 'gifts' and hope she would help others in a right way.

One rainy, stormy night, I went into labor. My baby girl was being born. Tessa carried me to the hospital while Jonathan was on his way. Moments after arriving at the emergency room, I had a beautiful little dark-skinned baby with thick black hair. She was the most gorgeous being that I had ever seen! I loved her instantly! As Tessa and I gleamed over this bundle of joy, I was worried as to why Jonathan hadn't arrived. I decided to name my baby girl, Terri Leigh, calling her Leigh. Her middle name was the same as her father's middle name.

While I rested, the baby was sent to the nursery. Tessa remained with me to keep a close watch on me. She was afraid I would have the same fate as my birthmother. I assured her I was fine, just needed to sleep awhile.

The next morning when I awoke, the nurse was bringing my little girl into the room. After preparations on feeding her, I finally got the hang of it. It was a magical moment. Tessa was just returning from the cafeteria with a tray full of breakfast when I gave the baby back to the nurse. After the nurse left taking my little girl back the nursery, Tessa sadly explained to me that Jonathan was killed late last night.

I screamed in pain as I felt my heart rip into. How could this happen?! Tessa held my hand in comfort as she called for a nurse to give me something strong. Later that evening, I awoke. I was still saddened and upset, but this time I seemed a little calm. Tessa was still beside me on my hospital bed when she told me what happened to Jonathan.

"Now child, becalm. Your husband was killed by a man in a hoodie. He broke into the coffeeshop and robbed him, shooting him two times in his chest. While you were sleeping that night, he was brought into the emergency room. I wouldn't let them wake you up, so I went down to see him, but he was already deceased. I'm so sorry Terri."

Speechless, I just gazed at the window. My heart ached so much! Tessa kept speaking to me, but I vaguely listened. She continued about how I needed to be strong and raise my daughter. I knew she meant well for me, but I needed some time to grieve.

Days later, I returned to my grandmother's place on Royal Street after closing the coffeeshop. I placed a 'for sale' sign in the window shortly after my husband's funeral was over. It was simply too painful to return there.

I focused on Leigh and taking care of her, which brought me peace in my heart as I watched her grow into an adorable toddler. Tessa and I taught her many things about life and our gifts. I carried her to the library with me every day as I worked, she enjoyed looking at the different books.

So, you have my small tale of how I became who I am. I still live in the French Quarter with my grandmother. Leigh is doing wonderfully in school and loves her 'spell' time when she gets home every day. She cares for my owl that I named Steve. She loves that animal!

I know one day, I will tell her about the 'curse' and it will be passed onto her, but for now we live happily and carry on.

The End.

Chapter 2: The Gothic Lady (Love Story) by Jo Jo Gray (Contributed by Jo Ann Atcheson Gray)

I'm JoAnna Lynn. I'm petite with brown eyes and black, lengthy hair. I've always been smaller than most of the girls my age, but I manage. I'm still in high school but this should be my final year. Yes, I am a senior. I will be glad when this school year is over with. I just turned eighteen a few weeks ago, so, I'm ready to leave my parent's house and start a new life of my own.

Some would call me 'gothic', but I feel like I'm just a normal girl with 'dark' desires. Somedays I feel misunderstood, especially by my parents and most of the teenagers at school. I usually stay to myself until some punk or jerk wants to try and 'pick' on me. Then I lose my temper a little and get sent home for three days. Don't mistaken me, I try to avoid any kind of conflict or arguments, but sometimes it just isn't an option.

I grew up in Central Alabama, a Southern state. I suppose I would be considered a country girl, yet I do not think I am. I've always felt I was born in the wrong town. I was not interested in the boys at my school and the girls were too 'shiny' for me. They played sports and hung out on weekends drinking beer and talking about hunting while the girls dreamed of marriage and such. I merely dreamed of leaving and seeing new places. My only hobby consisted of growing roses, mostly black and burgundy ones. I loved the roses of these colors! I planted several in my backyard and I talk to them on a daily basis. The other teenagers in town think I'm 'weird' but I don't mind. Only my roses comfort my dark soul.

I wasn't always so dark in appearance. It all began when my mother passed away last year. The pain and the sadness in my heart was unbearable, so I covered my sorrow with darkness. It was better than going into a deep depression. My father's new wife is nice, but I still cannot accept her. She wants me to be more like her with name brand clothes and stylish haircuts. I continuously refuse.

One rainy school day is when I met him, Christopher. He was adorable, different than the other guys. He was from New Orleans and just moved here with his uncle. He was tall and slender with dark brown hair that hung over his left eye, which were a bright blue. He wore blue jeans with holes in the knees and black t-shirts. He was a quiet guy with a mysterious character.

After bumping into him in the hallway and knocking my books to the floor, it all started from there. I knew I wanted him! His smile brightened my dark heart! As days went on, Christopher and I began to get closer to each other. We hung out all the time, mostly at his uncle's house, watching scary movies, listening to crazy music, and eating whatever we decided to be good at the time. I felt a slight happiness arise within me whenever he was around. He expressed to me how much he loved my attire and my way of dressing.

I often wore silly clothes such as evening gowns of dark colors with combat boots, and I usually kept mt hair piled messy on the top of my head. Normally, I would keep a black rose in my hair or whatever color I felt that day. My makeup was also darker, especially on my eyes. I felt safe, like no one could really see me behind my makeup.

Christopher would make promises of leaving this town and taking me with him. He swore to me that after graduation he would get me out of this place so we could be happy. I strangely believed him. My father did not care for him, but I didn't give a shit. Christopher was mine and we were going to be together.

My father would preach to me about Christopher and how he was just going to hurt me, but I knew he was only worried since he may lose his daughter to someone else. My father often drilled me about 'drugs' and 'sex' but I already knew of such things! I assure you I did not do drugs, but the sex I did do with Christopher. It was safe and of course I knew how to keep from getting pregnant. I wasn't stupid! I was a girl who hated alcohol, so parties were not on my agenda.

Several months blew by and Christopher bought a car. It was an old mustang that his uncle helped him purchase for his nineteenth birthday. It was bright red which made me gag but at least it rode good. On the weekends, we would venture to various places and explore different parks and movie theaters. It was such a nice time in my life!

When school finally ended and it was time for me to graduate, I did not go. I waited for my diploma to come in the mail. I was too busy with Christopher and making our preparations to leave. We agreed on going to his hometown in New Orleans. He explained to me that his grandmother, called Susie, lived in the French Quarter on the end of Royal Street. I was so excited to see a new place!

After intense arguments with my father, I finally won. So, me and Christopher loaded our baggage and set out for the French Quarter. I couldn't wait to see this place and meet Susie! Christopher assured me that his grandmother was going to love me! He told me all about her on the ride.

When we arrived that late evening at his grandmother's place in the French Quarter, it was amazing! It was an old dwelling yet beautiful. Susie owned a novelty shop with various trinkets of all sorts. There were incense sticks to tie dyed shirts for tourists. After meeting Susie, I knew I was where I wanted to be. She was a small, framed lady of seventy years old with thick blonde hair piled on her head. She wore old dresses of antique design and many bangle bracelets. Her fingers were covered in faded stone rings of different colors.

After being in the French Quarter for several weeks, I grew accustomed to the ways of this place. I started a job in Christopher's grandmother's shop while he went offshore on an oil rig to work. He would return home after a few months at a time then leave again. It took some getting used to.

I was strangely happy! Susie taught me many different cultures and the history of the French Quarter. I was intrigued at the start! My favorite practices were the 'spells' and different herbal remedies. I wasn't any good with them, but it was still awesome to be a part of something.

I never liked playing with the dark magic though, it frightened me. Susie would assure me that it was fine to be cautious of such things and she never forced me to partake in those rituals.

I would meet many strangers and several locals while running the shop on a daily routine. I enjoyed talking with the people who lived here and hearing their experiences. Often my father would call and see how I was doing, and I would tell him I'm good. I never talked too long to him but at times I did miss him.

The last time I saw Christopher was the stormy night after he returned from work. We were alone in the shop while Susie slept. Christopher had purchased a small diamond ring with a black band, asking me to marry him. I said 'yes' immediately. As the days carried on, we planned our small ceremony. We were going to be married in front of the Saint Louis Cathedral by his grandmother, who was also ordained.

It was a dream come true! The wedding was simple yet amazing, romantic! I wore a white dress with lace for the first time! I had white feathers of silk throughout my piled-up hair and flip flops with pearls across the straps. My makeup was still heavy and dark. I felt like a princess! My dark soul was brightened during this time.

Our honeymoon consisted of a weekend in St. Francisville at the Myrtles Plantation. It was an adventure! This mansion was terrifying yet gorgeous. I enjoyed the tour of the place and all the tales that went along with it. We stayed on the top floor in one of the bedrooms. It was quite spooky, but I knew I was safe with Christopher. We made passionate love that night while unexplainable bumps and sounds rang throughout the house! I was so happy!

When we returned to the French Quarter on that Monday morning, Christopher had to leave again and return to his job. I was saddened but I knew I would see him in a few weeks. I was wrong!

Some days later, Susie received a call from the manager on Christopher's oil rig. Christopher was killed by an explosion on the rig. He was instantly deceased.

Susie screamed in pain as I hit my knees behind the counter, crying as hard as I could. My heart hurt so bad! This was so much more painful than when my mother passed away. Instantly, I withdrew myself back into my darkness.

After a while, the funeral procession was set, and everyone paraded down the cobblestone streets as we ventured to the graveyard to place Christopher at rest. It was a heart-breaking day!

Later that night, I discovered a note on my pillow from Susie...

Sweet JoAnna Lynn,

I have grown to love you as my own child. Hope you will carry on and live a wonderful, fulfilled life. I feel my time has come to leave this world and enter the afterlife with my Christopher and his precious mother. The shop is now yours; I've left all the paperwork under the counter in the front parlor for you. Live well, my dear and keep your spirit fresh.

Susie

I was dumbfounded after reading this. I bolted to Susie's bedroom only to find her lifeless across her bed with a bottle of anti-depressants on the side table that was empty.

Another funeral to attend and I had Susie placed next to Christopher in the cemetery. I was in a deep depression by this point. I felt so alone! I knew I would stay in the French Quarter and continue to run Susie's shop, yet I felt abandoned, left behind!

A few weeks slipped by, and I discovered I was expecting a child. I controlled my depression by focusing on my baby being born. The day she arrived was beautiful! She had curly brown hair and bright blue eyes and favored her daddy quite a bit. I named her Susanna Christie. I would always honor Susie and Christopher by naming our child after them.

Time continued on as I raised my daughter here in the French Quarter. My father and his absurd wife came on many occasions to visit and see their grandchild. Susanna Christie loved them so much!

I continued to wear dark vintage clothes while I dressed my baby girl in pastel colors with lace. She was an amazing toddler and very smart! I taught all the herbal remedies that Susie had taught me, and she was quite good at performing her 'magic'. She adopted a few cats of different colors as her pets and enjoyed playing with them. They would even sleep next to her at bedtime.

So, you have my little story of my simple life. I dwell in the French Quarter still with my daughter who has grown into an amazing woman. Susanna Christie now has children of her own, four sons and one daughter, and a husband who is in the medical field. They live only miles from me outside of the French Quarter. My father passed away some months back with cancer while his awful wife moved on.

I spend my days at my shop while playing and enjoying my grandchildren on a regular routine. Life hasn't been perfect, but it has its special moments. I will carry on exactly the way Susie said in her final note to me.

The Gothic Lady

(Love Story)

Chapter 3: Seductions of a Vampire by Anna Elizabeth

Lust. Such a small word with so much meaning and feeling attached to it. It can make one forget all their worries and fears. It can make one forget about being alone and being immortal.

I'm Anna Leigh Grace, most call me Grace. I am such a being as this. I think of the word 'talent', and I've realized you cannot pick your talents, your talents pick you. Some may call me wicked or bad, but I just merely survive. I do what I must to stay alive in this undead body, but a small amount of 'fun' keeps me from getting too bored. Immortality is a very long time.

This is my little tale...

I was transformed at the age of seventeen in the early 1800's. I've lived the undead life for a long while. I had to learn my own way with this transformation. My maker was an old man with white hair that ran off after making me. I never saw him again, even now, I think he's dead, but I can't be sure.

It all began one rainy night in New Orleans, in what is now considered to be the French Quarter. My Aunt ran the local brothel, and I was under her care since the death of my parents. They were brutally murdered by a wolf outside of New Orleans while hunting in the woods. My mother always went with my father on his hunts. She would always tell me to be strong and learn to do what the men do, so you can always take care of yourself. I was only ten years old when they were massacred in the woods.

As I mentioned earlier, I was seventeen when I was changed into an immortal being. I worked in the bar area along with a chubby gentleman that was bald and smelled weird. He taught me all the ways of making strong drinks and the proper ways to pour a shot of whiskey. While my aunt managed the 'girls' of the evening.

I was a quiet girl, yet I paid close attention to my surroundings, learning all I could about running a brothel such as this. Sometimes the paying gentleman would get rowdy, and my aunt would scream for the chubby man behind the bar to toss them out into the cobblestone streets. Of course, my aunt would express to the gentlemen that I was strictly off limits. I was far too young at the time to be about the main floor mingling with the men.

As I said, it was a rainy night when I was changed forever. I was dwelling behind the bar as usual when a bearded man of much age with long white hair entered through the swinging doors. The place was lacking in customers this night and I was working the bar alone while the chubby, bald bartender was taking a nap in the backroom. My aunt was upstairs in her room doing whatever she usually does when it's slow on the main floor.

This bearded man eased to the counter speaking in a low rough tone ordering a shot of our strongest whiskey. I noticed he gazed around the room before taking his shot. He seemed mysterious and rough in appearance, yet he also seemed intriguing. His eyes were dark and sad. He had such a mystery about him!

I was a prideful little thing, so I had to make a conversation with this stranger! I knew I should've minded my own business but where was the 'fun' in doing that?

"So, mister, what brings you in this town?" I asked seductively.

Not answering me, this man pointed to his shot glass for more whiskey. Pouring him another round, I spoke again but with a slight amount of boldness, "I asked you a question, sir."

This gentleman grunted at me and swallowed his whiskey slamming the shot glass back onto the counter. He spoke in a low tone, "Have a round on me, pretty lady."

Quickly, I grabbed another shot glass and poured us a round of whiskey. If my Aunt caught me drinking, I knew I'd be in a heap of trouble, but I did not care. This was exciting to me, yet I knew it could be dangerous due to the fact this was a complete stranger.

After a few rounds of whiskey and flirtatious conversation with this bearded man, I lost my memory. I awoke in my bed upstairs with a horrible pain in my neck and a severe headache. My Aunt was sitting next to me with my hand in hers. She appeared to be worried and anxious.

"What happened?" I managed to whisper.

"I'm not exactly sure, Grace." My Aunt replied. "I found you behind the bar knocked completely out with a cut or something on your neck. You were bleeding. So, I quickly called for the doctor. He hadn't any idea why you were bleeding on your neck unless you had cut yourself somehow. That's when the doctor suggested I take you upstairs and put you in bed to rest."

After days of being in bed, I was miserable. The sun that peaked through my window was aggravating me. It pained my eyes! My neck was still sore, but it was bearable. My pour Aunt had no idea what was wrong with me, and the doctor visited a few more times. He was also clueless to my condition. I was fevered and sweating an awful lot, I became fearful. Then I realized that strange, bearded gentleman must have done something to me.

A few nights passed; I was getting worse. My Aunt tried to comfort me, but it was useless. I was feeling like a crazy animal, restless. I had a weird hunger to taste blood. That very night, I became a monster! I attacked my Aunt draining her of all her blood. I was so afraid of myself after that.

I massacred everyone downstairs including the bald bartender. I ran away into the woods to hide myself from the lawmen that searched the brothel. I cried so hard when I noticed my tears were merely blood tears. 'Why did I kill my only family?'

After months went by, I returned to the brothel, but it was abandoned. I claimed to the lawmen, that the white haired, bearded man was the one who did the killings, and I ran away in fear. My story was believable to them. Finally, after months of searching for this man, the lawmen gave up and closed the case. I remained at the brothel house.

Eventually over time, I realized what I was. A vampire, a creature of the night. I was the myth that I had heard stories about, and that bearded man was the one who did this to me. He was obviously a vampire, an undead being. It took me a hard lesson to understand that the sunlight was fatal to me, but I quickly learned. I knew the town people said evil things about me, but I did not care. I stayed in this place only venturing out late at night to fulfill my blood lust, taking only one person a night to sustain my cravings. I had to be discreet, or the lawmen would catch me. So, I managed to make my killings look accidental.

Over the centuries, the town changed quite a bit, and I remained in this brothel house. Now, it's a hotel in the heart of the French Quarter. I have others running the place and I only show my presence on small occasions. As the centuries dragged on, I learned more about what kind of fiend I was. I became quite good at surviving and seducing the men that would pass through getting my blood fill yet not murdering them. Some I killed and some I would let them live to see another day.

I became comfortable in this new century. I grew accustomed to their apparel, blue jeans and a tank top with boots. I kept my long, dark hair clipped high on my head. Often times, I would wear a fancy lace dress made of black silk with a Mardi Gra mask of pure black, silk lace on my face when I would parade the cobblestone streets of the French Quarter at night. I would mingle in and out of the bars on Bourbon Street casually flirting with individuals that caught my interest. Most of the people dressed in this fashion, especially the locals, just merely to entertain the tourists.

This place has changed so much since the early 1800's! Now one can merely express oneself no matter the craziness of how it looks. There are always parades and exciting events happening on a regular basis. Even funerals are thrilling! It amazes me how everyone strolls down the cobblestone streets dancing and singing on their way to the cemetery just outside the French Quarter only to lay their loved one to rest.

My victims are usually easy to seduce, especially on Bourbon Street. It's simple to lure an individual aside just long enough to taste their blood and get my fill for the night since they are so drunken on alcohol. Some nights, my victims were rough so I would lure them to a close dark alleyway and devour them. It usually depended on their attitude toward me whether I drained them completely or not. I grew accustomed with the ways of the younger crowd, the young adults. All they wanted to do was party until daylight. I didn't mind since I had to be gone before then. Some nights, I just played around and seduced whoever was interested without actually biting them. It really depended on my mood. I always wore my silk mask whether I dressed up or not. I did not want anyone to remember my face.

One late night, I was toying with a guy with braids that hung over his shoulders. His muscle tone was fascinating. I longed for his blood on my tongue. We were dancing and sipping on some kind of fruity drink when I caught a glimpse of a man across the room. This man was leaned against the bar looking straight at me. He was tall with a sense of uniqueness. After losing interest in the braided hair guy, I merely just walked away from him. He kept dancing as if I was never there. Lucky for him, he wouldn't be dying tonight. My focus was now on the stranger at the bar.

Cautiously, I approached this serious looking man and said, "How about buying a girl a drink?"

He replied, "No thanks. I'd rather step outside where it's quiet and have a conversation."

Following this guy out of the bar, I was curious as to who he was and why he wanted to talk to me. I kept trying to decide if I should just kill him, but my curiosity wanted to know what he wanted with me.

When we reached a quiet destination, I noticed this man was wearing a pistol on his side. I knew he had to be a part of some kind of law enforcement. I was correct.

"I've been searching for you for days now. Are you Grace?" this man asked.

"Yes, that's my name? Why are you looking for me?" I questioned seriously.

"I'm with the National Service of Law and I'm investigating a series of murders in this area. You were mentioned by witnesses that you might have some clues for me. Shall we discuss some things?" He answered sternly.

I agreed and we began walking along the side of the street as this man explained in detail about the horrible murders over the last year. He told me how they were found drained of their blood and evidence was collected that led him to me. The majority of the victims were found behind my hotel in an alleyway, and some were located behind some of the bars on Bourbon Street.

I knew exactly what he was describing since I was the one who did them, I just got sloppy in my feedings, I suppose. Of course, I denied knowing anything about them. There was something about this man that intrigued me. I did want to kill him just yet. So, I listened and play along. It was a good thing that I decided not to wear my mask tonight, I only wore jeans and a t-shirt with flip-flops tonight.

"Exactly what is your name, sir?" I asked in a low mumble.

"I'm Detective Alex, and I need some answers from you, Miss Grace."

"I do not know anything, sir. I'm just a simple girl running a hotel, who likes to party and mingle with the tourists on nightly routine." I confessed in a shy way.

Once we reached the bench across from the St. Louis Cathedral, we sat down. It was getting late, and I was getting bored. This detective commenced in telling me that he traced all the evidence back to me. Apparently, they found pieces of black lace and a pearl stone on one of the victims. The local residents expressed how I was the only one they had seen wearing that type of lace and such on a mask upon my face. The residents told this detective of how I was quiet and mysterious and so on. I was becoming frustrated while he continued his story.

Alex explained in detail how he discovered from historic records about what is possibly my ancestors from this area. It was my great, great Aunt, he believes, that was the first owner of my building, yet it was a type of saloon and brothel back then. She had adopted her young niece and raised her in this place. It was surprisingly coincidental that I looked exactly like that niece. He wanted to know how I became the owner of my hotel and more about my family history since he discovered my Aunt and everyone at the brothel house was massacred and drained of all their blood, and no one was ever prosecuted for the murders. Only the young girl survived, and no one knew what happened to her afterwards. It was too similar to the murders of late not to look into it. It was labeled as 'vampire-style murders' and he was confused as to how and why. He also told me that there was always a single black rose nicely placed on the victims.

I was speechless when he finally stopped talking. I wanted to rip his throat out, but I just couldn't. His eyes were a dark brown and his shaggy brown hair draped across his eye. He was adorable to me! Besides, I knew that single black rose was placed on them by me. I had an obsession with black roses lately, so I thought it 'romantic' to leave one on my victims.

When he mentioned that he was going to have to take me into the station for more questioning, I disappeared. I left him looking in all directions for me while cursing out loud. I wasn't going to jail or anywhere. I did not want to hurt him, but he needed to back off.

Reaching my hotel, I went straight to my suite and locked the door. I would deal with this mess tomorrow night. The sun would be coming up soon and I needed rest. I figured I would feed first thing tomorrow evening and then go in search of this detective named Alex. I knew I'd better be discreet on who and where I fed, so I decided no more killing my victims until this investigation was over.

The next night after sunset, I ventured out to find my meal for the evening. I had to feed, or I would end up biting the detective. I walked to a nearby alley and chose a homeless man who was sound asleep against the damp building. Leaving him propped nicely against the old building, I realized he was dead. Placing a single black rose with a black satin ribbon tied around it on his dirty chest, I spoke out loud in a low tone with a hint of sarcasm, "My mistake, I did not mean to do that! Maybe, this ribbon tied to the rose will confuse my lawman. Oh well, now to find the detective."

Passing back by my hotel on my way to the police station, Alex was already standing next to the front entrance with a small note pad in his hands. I was wearing my jeans and a revealing white tank top with a black lace bra along with my combat boots when I approached him. I knew better than to wear my mask right now.

"Follow me, sir. "I said boldly as I passed by him on my way inside the hotel.

He followed me all the way to my suite as I motioned for him to come in and have a seat. It was now or never. I had to handle this detective now or things were going to get out of hand.

"Would you like anything to drink, sir?" I asked in a growl as I smiled at him.

Not answering me, Alex only gazed about my room as if he was investigating it. That's when I noticed he was staring at the single black rose on my dinette table. It was wrapped with a black satin ribbon. I had forgotten to hide that little piece of evidence before bringing him to my dwelling.

Before he could stand and say anything, I was quickly in his face with my hands holding his chin. I explained to him that there was only two ways to survive this situation. One, he could simply leave and never come back. Two, he could make passionate 'love' to me then leave and never come again!

I kissed his lips hard and felt a lustful surge run through my entire undead body. Strangely, Alex gave in and kissed me back. Leading him to the bedroom, we began taking off all our clothing and was intertwined across my bed. It was amazing! He made 'love' to me hard and angry.

Afterwards, Alex spoke sternly as he smiled at me, "I'm still arresting you for the murders of several people, Miss Grace."

He began reading me my rights as he put his clothes back on. Reaching in his pocket of his jeans, he pulled out a set of handcuffs.

"At least let me get dressed first, sir." I said while I chuckled a small laugh.

Nodding in head in agreement, I quickly dressed. I walked over to him with my wrists in front of me gesturing for him to place the handcuffs. Before he tried putting them on me, I revealed my fangs to him. He jumped back in fear as he tried to exit my room. Pulling his gun from his side, he raised it as if to shoot me, but I was already on him. Tossing the gun away, I held him strongly so he could not move. Looking him in his eyes, I said, "I am the myth you heard about, and those murders were done by a real 'Vampire'. I am the niece in the historic tale you read about. I am Anna Leigh Grace. You sir, are about to meet your maker tonight."

Sinking my fangs deep into his flesh, I drained him until there wasn't any blood left in his body. I felt awful, but it had to be done. He was simply too curious about me. I really liked this detective though and he could make one feel so good during intercourse. It was an awful shame to have to end his life.

After midnight, I discreetly exposed of his body in the river. I even shed a single blood tear for him as his body drifted away down the Mississippi River. Another unsolved missing person to wash up later and become an unsolved murder case.

As time passed, I continued my usual routine of running the hotel. I only fed twice a week now so as not to cause any attention. I mostly began feeding on the 'bad' people in this area, who would rob or try to hurt some of the tourists. I still think about the detective on occasion and wish it could've been different. I could've 'loved' this Alex if he hadn't been so determined to convict me of murder.

So, this was my small tale of how I became immortal and my strange existence. I still remain in the French Quarter, even now. I still run my hotel, yet my appearance is slightly different. I discovered the art of coloring my hair in a regular manner. It's always a different color, at least every year, I change it. Of course, I continue to wear a mask from time to time, except it varies in style and color. I still keep my original satin black mask in my suite locked in a drawer just so I can remember Alex. I continue to leave a single black rose on my victims and most of the time, I will wear one in my piled-up hair just for fun.

Maybe, someday I will cross paths with you while you are visiting the French Quarter or staying in my beautiful hotel.

Keep your eyes open for me... 'Grace'

Seductions of a Vampire

Chapter 4: A Black Rose Murder by Anna Elizabeth

Do you believe in 'ghosts'? Well, I used to believe in facts. There was always an explanation for strange happenings, until I witnessed my first sighting of an actual spirit. I'm Jessica Anne. This is my small tale of how I spoke with a ghost and the story of how she was murdered.

It all started on a bright sunshine day. I met my friends at the creek in Central Alabama. It was a small creek with just enough water to relax and splash around in. At the age of eighteen and just out of high school, I enjoyed hanging out with my fellow students. The summer had just begun, and it was extremely hot. While I reclined on a blanket on the banks of the creek, my friends played and tossed around in the water. I loved to feel the sun on my slightly tanned skin. Thats when my companions decided to venture down the creek. They begged me to go along, but I was too comfortable resting in the sun for such an adventure.

After they had disappeared down the creek, it was silent, peaceful. I could hear the birds chirping in the distance. About the time I dosed off in a relaxing slumber, I heard a woman's voice. It was faint and sounded like it came from the water. Jumping into a sitting position, I lowered my sunglasses searching for the voice I just heard. It sounded like someone was calling for 'help'. Looking in all directions, I did not see anyone.

Thinking to myself that I must be getting too hot and losing my mind, I decided to move to the water and cool off for a while. Laying in the cold water as it ran over my shoulders wetting my long dark hair, I heard the voice again. This time it was very clear, saying, "I need your help!"

Jumping to my feet, I looked near the edge of the water next to the trees and there she was, a ghost dressed in a black lace dress with a black blindfold around her eyes. She was holding a single black rose in her hands. I could actually see straight through her. Frozen in fear, I mumbled, asking, "Who are you and why do you need my help?"

I couldn't run or scream, I was too afraid at what I was seeing! As this entity gracefully moved toward me, I stumbled falling back into the water. This ghost reaches her hand out to me as if to help me up. Of course, I did not take her hand, I quickly gathered my wits about me and ran onto the sandy banks near the edge of the water. When I turned around in curiosity, she was right behind me. This time, I actually screamed out in fear! The ghost lady spoke, "Please, do not fear me. I must relate my tale to you."

That's when this spirit took my hand in hers and motioned for me to sit down. Fearfully, I sat onto the dirty ground as this ghost lady seated herself next to me. Still shaking, I asked her, "Who are you? What happened to you?"

"I am Katherine Marie. I want to tell you of my death."

Now I was even more afraid. As this ghost lady released my hand, I pondered whether to run away or stay to hear her story.

"You must not be afraid of me, girl. I will not harm you." Katherine assured me. "I only want my story to be known."

Calming my nerves, but only a slight bit, I waited for this ghost lady to begin her tale. I could see she was very ancient in her apparel, yet I wondered how she died, and why she wanted me to know. Noticing the marks around her neck, it seemed like someone cut her throat. I was extremely fearful, but I remained still, not moving as this ghost lady began her story...

"My name, as I said, is Katherine Marie. I was only nineteen when my life ended. I was in love with the man who lived in town. He was much older than I was, but in my time, it was favored to marry a wealthy, older gentleman. He owned the local bank in the middle of our town. He worked with my father on several local building projects, as my father was a carpenter. This gentleman asked my father for my hand in marriage, and my father agreed. I was thrilled when I was told my fate to this gentleman. His name was Charles. He was a well-respected man in our little community."

Interrupting this ghost lady, I asked, "How old were you when you died? What century did you live in?"

She responded, "Please, no interruptions, girl. I will explain these details to you."

Saying my apologies, Katherine continued her tale...

"After a beautiful, simple wedding, Charles and I ventured to this same little creek to have a romantic picnic before going to his place for the evening. I was excited since I was now his wife and later, I would become a woman. I couldn't wait to start a family and have children of my own. How was I to know that Charles had a different plan for me? When Charles spread the wool blanket across the ground in this very spot where we are sitting, I rested myself next to him. We kissed and talked for what seemed like hours. It was nearing sunset when my fate was decided. Charles told me he had a nice surprise for me. So, he blindfolded me and told me to wait. As I sat, waiting for my surprise, that's when I felt a horrible pain across my neck. When I awoke, I was alone, no one was around. I tried to venture home, but I only woke up in this same area, repeatedly. That's when I knew I was dead. As the memory of what happened filled my thoughts, I knew Charles had murdered me by slitting my throat with a dull knife. I pondered the same question over and over as to why he had done this to me. That's when I realized the reason why. Charles had made an investment with my father to inherit my life insurance, which at the time was worth $1000.00. Wasn't a fortune but in the early 1800's it was a lot of money. My father had willed my inheritance to Charles so he could invest it for my safe keeping. In that era, it wasn't allowed for a woman to handle such a large amount of money. As time lingered and I was haunting this creek, Charles returned to say 'good-bye' to me.

While he stood on the muddy banks of this creek, he said out loud to me as I watched from the trees, "So long, my beautiful Katherine Marie. I'm so sorry for what I did to you, but it had to be done. I'm leaving town now to start fresh in another place. I had to have your assets to begin my new life. Your parents are fully aware that you were attacked by Indians, and they brutally murdered you and took off with your body. Good-bye, my dear, may you rest in peace."

He left without shedding any sort of tears for me, he only tossed this black rose into the water. I was angered, yet saddened as I watched him disappear, knowing I could not follow him. I have haunted this creek for many years now and I never knew what happened to my murderous husband. Only some time ago, I learned the fate of my dear Charles. A woman came to visit this very area. She was tall and pretty with blonde hair. She had some children with her that looked to be around twelve years of age. She was showing them the creek and explaining to them that this was where their grandfather used to play when he was very young. She spoke his name calling him Grandpaw Charles. I put it all together and realized my husband, Charles, had continued his life and had children of his own. It grieved me greatly. I never saw that woman or those kids again. I've remained here for years just watching various people come and go. I decided it was time to reveal my story to someone, and I chose you, girl. I want you to tell my tale and let others know how I was sadly killed and never had the chance to live my life."

This ghost lady handed me the black rose she was holding, and she disappeared. At that moment, I heard my friends returning from down the creek. I could hear their laughter and such as they approached me. I was standing, speechless, holding this dead black rose in my hand when my one friend asked, "Where did you find a dead rose?"

Not answering her, I merely said, "I'm not sure where it came from. I'm going home since it's about to be dark."

Leaving my companions on the creek bed, I went straight home and turned on my computer. I searched the internet for hours in hopes of finding any clues to this sort of murder in this area. Finally, I came across some old newspapers online that was archived. It was clearly in front of my eyes! There she was, pictured in a nice fashioned dress wearing a floral hat with her dark hair neatly stacked. She was standing next to a tall man holding a top hat and a cane. It appeared to be a wedding photograph. Underneath the faded black and white picture was the headline, "Woman Massacred By Indians On Her Wedding Day".

I was speechless, this ghost lady was real! Her story was labeled as a brutal killing by Indians, yet I alone knew she was murdered by her husband.

Several months passed as I tried to relate Katherine's story to the people at the courthouse in the archived records, but no one would listen to me. They actually thought I was being insane and making up childish stories about the past. I went many times to the creek in search of the ghost lady, but never found her. She was gone! I suppose she revealed her tale and could finally rest in peace.

Over the years, I grew into a respectable woman and married having two lovely girls of my own. I moved away from Central Alabama and started my life with my husband in New York City. I named my first-born girl, Maria Katherine. I never told anyone of my ghostly encounter, yet I often thought of her. I began a career as a journalist and published a small newspaper article about Katherine Marie. Of course, no one would believe my story, yet I felt it was the right thing to do for her. Now, her story can be known forever. I still have the dead black rose in a photo album and I look it often as to keep the ghost lady, Katherine Marie, and her memory alive. May she for all eternity, Rest in Peace!

A Black Rose Murder

Chapter 5: "Jo Jo" (A Memoir) by Anna Elizabeth

Sometimes friends can be more like family, yet one would gladly lay down one's life if it meant saving them. I had such a friend as this. I'm Josie and this is my little tale about 'Jo Jo', my one true friend. My memories of her and our short years together. I am immortal now, but I wasn't undead at the time of meeting Jo Jo. It was sometime after our meeting each other that I was turned by a male vampire at a carnival in town. Jo Jo never feared me, yet it was a while before she actually believed I was a vampire. It all came to light for her one rainy night when she saw me feed on a person, but that's to be told later.

I would like to start my little memoir of Jo Jo on the day I met her. I was in school, only eleventh grade, a junior, when she arrived in my class, which was literature. She was new in town and didn't know anybody. She had moved here from California, so adjusting to southern living was a slight struggle for her. Moving from San Francisco to a small town in Central Alabama was extremely different. At the age of sixteen, we both were clueless to the struggles life would toss our way. I was a petite girl with fair skin, brown eyes and wavy short hair. Jo Jo was beautiful with her long blonde hair and green eyes and tanned skin. She was taller than me and very outgoing in character. She enjoyed flirting with the guys, and she loved to 'party' on a regular basis. Jo Jo would often laugh at my southern accent, but it was fine, I knew she loved it.

Anyway, back to when I first met her...

Like I said, I first saw her when she entered my classroom that day. She seated herself in the desk next to mine. I tried to keep from staring at her but there was just something about this new girl. She noticed my gaze and winked her eye at me. Nervously, I turned my attention back to the teacher who was talking about Shakespeare.

Later that morning, as I was eating my lunch in the cafeteria, Jo Jo walked up to my table asking if she could join me. Of course, I said yes to her request.

Long story short, our friendship started from there... We were inseparable after that.

As months passed, Jo Jo made me attend many 'parties' with the seniors of our school. She introduced me to alcohol, which I did not enjoy the day after. She taught me how to properly wear makeup and how to fix my hair in a stylish fashion. She even changed my style of clothes to match hers. I have to admit, she helped me come out of my shell. Although, I refused to wear bright colors of clothing, she accepted the fact, and I still wore my denim jeans with holes in the knees. We were different as night and day, but it worked for us!

Jo Jo loved to be the center of attention when we were at the parties, yet I never wanted to be. I would hang back in the shadows while she did her thing impressing the other guys that stood around. She was such an outgoing person, and she enjoyed socializing. She always had her hair and makeup fixed perfectly, even on the slowest of days. Jo Jo would always grumble at me since I hated to wear makeup and most of the time I clipped my hair up on top of my head, not wanting to even brush it.

Memories of Jo Jo were exciting as she taught me many things about socializing and mingling with other teenagers our age. She showed different ways to take care of myself without having to ever have a job. I must confess, her methods were unorthodox, but they worked. I, personally, would rather have a job! One some occasions, Jo Jo would entertain adults by seducing the man and take his money. I hated that side of her, but she never forced me to do anything in that manner.

We went to several concerts in the city, listening to our favorite rock bands and on some occasions, we would go to 'rap' shows which Jo Jo loved. She would dance and act a fool while smiling at me. I would always laugh at her. She would always tell me to just enjoy life, because you never know when it will come to an end. I tried to follow in her footsteps but at times, she seemed beyond my abilities. I wasn't such a person to do what she did! I never judged her ways, yet sometimes I worried she would go too far and get in a world of mess!

One such night, we attended the local carnival in the city. Everything was going well, and we were having a wonderful time riding the rides, which I did not like too well, when she noticed an older gentleman with a faded top hat standing alone behind the roller-coaster. Of course, Jo Jo had to investigate and see who this mysterious guy was. She ventured in his direction while I slowly walked a few steps behind her, I kept telling her not to bother this man, but she didn't listen. After starting a conversation, this strange gentleman invited us to a small gathering at his dwelling outside of the carnival. I strongly urged Jo Jo to say no, but she never acknowledged me. Reluctantly, I followed Jo Jo to this man's place. It was a little camper on the outskirts of the city. This guy invited us in while he prepared some alcoholic beverages for us.

I did not attempt to drink anything this man offered to us, but Jo Jo was sipping on the first drink when I noticed this weird guy placed a white powdery substance on the little table in front of us. Needless to say, it was drugs! Jo Jo did not hesitate; she snorted this powder like she knew what she was doing! I was mind-blown! I had never seen her try drugs before! The strange man never did any of that powdery stuff, he only watched Jo Jo do it. He offered it to me, but I kindly said no! In fact, I told Jo Jo that we needed to leave! She did not listen to me! I was afraid to leave her here alone, so I stayed.

After several hours, Jo Jo was passed out on the little couch while I just sat there staring at this man. He never drank anything, and he was very mysterious. After a few minutes, he asked me, "So, you must be the cautious one?"

I did not reply to him, I only began trying to wake Jo Jo up so we could get the hell away from this scary man, but there was no getting her awake. This man said as he grinned an evil grin at me, "You are more than welcome to crash here until your friend awakes, my dear."

That's when this man stood and came closer to me. I was very fearful.

The next morning, I awoke to find myself and Jo Jo lying on a damp wooden bench in the local park. I was oblivious of what happened with that strange guy! We never seen him again.

As the days went on, I was becoming very sensitive to the sunlight. I felt my skin tingle every time I went outside my house. I kept expressing my symptoms to Jo Jo but she would only chuckle and say I was being a wimp. I tried to talk to her about that weird guy, but she would say "Get over it, Josie. It was just a small party on one night."

Just to sum it all up, I was becoming a Vampire! Jo Jo thought I was going insane! She did not believe me, until that one night, when I actually took a stranger's life.

Jo Jo and I went to the movie theater to watch the newest horror film. While in our seats, this woman set next us since the seats were filled all around the place. I caught a scent of her blood, and it began from there! I cautiously attacked this woman without anyone noticing, draining her of all her blood in her body. Jo Jo noticed.

After we returned to Jo Jo's place, I tried to tell her what I was and that I believed that strange man from the carnival did this to me! She was furious yet calm. I tried to explain to her that I fully believed this guy wanted to do it to her but she passed out. I'm not sure why this male vampire didn't kill us, but I was thankful we were still alive! It will forever be a mystery since I never saw this fiend again!

Months passed and Jo Jo accepted the fact that I was now immortal. She became accustomed to me only venturing out at night, and on the nights, I had to feed on a person, she would linger away from me until I was finished. I tried on many occasions, to get her to let me try and change her into what I was, but she only refused me. She would tell me that she may have bad habits, but killing someone for their blood wasn't for her.

Jo Jo kept my secret of immortality and she never complained. She only proceeded with her normal routine of partying on a nightly basis. Of course, we both dropped out of school since there wasn't any way I could attend during the daylight hours. After we turned eighteen years of age, we moved into our own apartment in the city. It was a small dwelling yet comfortable. My victims I fed on would kindly give me the funds to pay our rent and whatever we needed. Jo Jo continued to live her life through parties while I existed on a lower level. I rarely attended her parties when she would have them in our apartment, I would leave for the night only to come in before the sun rose and find Jo Jo passed out somewhere in the place.

One night, Jo Jo had a party inviting many of the local high school friends of hers. As usual, I simply left until the party was over. When I arrived home that stormy night, I found Jo Jo in the bathtub unconscious, naked, and not breathing! Quickly, I tried to wake her but it was no such luck. I thought about trying to bite her in hopes of turning her, but it was too late. Jo Jo was gone!

After calling the paramedics, and they removed her body from our apartment, I was told by the male nurse that my friend had overdosed on some type of drug.

I only had Jo Jo in my life for a few short years, but we were close like 'sisters'. I will never forget her and the memories we shared. Some nights it's hard when I think of Jo Jo. If only she would've let me make her into what I am! Jo Jo will always be a cherished memory!

Years have gone by, and I am still here in Central Alabama. I traveled for a while and saw many places. I remain immortal yet I do not socialize with anyone. I stay in the shadows except when I have to venture out and fill my bloodlust. I still dwell in our apartment yet it's hard some nights due to all the memories of Jo Jo. I have her portrait on my wall above my bed. An artist in Italy painted it for me from an old photograph I keep in a locket around my neck.

So, you have my little tale of Jo Jo. It wasn't much, but her memory means a lot to me. I talk to her portrait mostly every night as if she's still here. This vast eternity seems unbearable at times without her, yet I manage. Life threw a struggle upon me, yet I refuse to stop existing. I will remain undead until my time comes to leave this eternity.

Forever in my undead, cold heart... In memory of a 'friend' that once was...

"Jo Jo" (A Memoir)

❖

Chapter 6: The Vampire's Betrayal by Sasha Joy

The Vampire's Betrayal

Part 1: Lust Games

Desire... the one thing I crave more than blood. Lust and money can become an addiction. The feeling of pleasure to one's own body can make one forget all the emptiness, the loneliness, and the eternal damnation of one's soul, if my soul still exists. The ecstasy of the warm blood as it runs down my throat, as I hear the faint beating of my victim's heart. This is my story...

Being immortal has its moments of being victorious, yet it brings such guilt for a short moment. I'm Veronica. I am an immortal such as this. I'm currently residing in Manhattan, New York within the luxurious walls of The Ritz-Carlton Hotel near Times Square, practically living in room 704. The surrounding attractions lure tourists to this massive abode, such as the Empire State Building, the Museum of Modern Art, and many other nice restaurants where the wealthy can throw their money away. This location is exactly where my story begins, where I do my best seductions, and where I find my prey.

Being petite and beautiful with brown, wavy hair barely touching my shoulder and eyes of the purest green, I taunt the tourists as they pass through in this little hotel bar. Basically, it's a nightly routine. I patiently wait for someone who is alone and looks to be slightly rich. I sip my wine in a fancy glass, although it has a bittersweet taste, as I watch the people come and go. Unfortunately, I cannot read their thoughts, that's the one undead gift I do not possess. Dwelling at the mahogany bar with the dim lights above, I cautiously scan the small crowd of drunken individuals.

One such person catches my eye. He's a distinguished gentleman that looks to be in his late forties. His frame appears to be slightly muscular underneath his dark blue, tailored suit with hair as black as night. He seems average yet expensive as he drinks his bourbon on ice. He must be a man of some importance. Gently picking my wine glass up, I flirtatiously stroll over to his table. Our eyes meet as I place myself across from him...

"So, are you visiting or are you here on business?" I seductively ask as I continue to look into his eyes sipping my red wine.

Coughing a nervous cough, he answered in an Italian accent, "Just business, pretty lady. May I ask who you are?"

"I'm Veronica, sir," I replied. "I can make your wildest dreams a reality, at least for one evening."

Smiling, the man nodded his head and asked, "Exactly, how are you supposed to do that? Besides, you look to be about twenty years of age."

"Trust me, sir, I'm well beyond twenty years old." I stated as I grinned an evil grin taking another sip of my bitter wine.

It wasn't much longer into this petty conversation, I had him in my grasp.

Caressing in a heated, lustful passion, we made our way up to the seventh floor to my suite. Passing through the hotel door to my spacious room, clothes began coming off. This man's intense body was stunning! His muscle tone was almost perfect. As he stared lustfully into my green eyes, I slowly pushed him onto the queen-sized bed with satin sheets. Climbing on top of his well-toned form, I straddled his hard, masculine manliness. He groaned in pleasure as I forcefully squeezed my thighs into him. I began to caress his bare chest with my fingertips as I leaned into his strong embrace. His massive arms held my naked, cold body against his warm, male physique. Slowly and playfully, I commenced kissing his neck in the area I intended on piercing with my sharp teeth. Thrusting harder as I held him in my grasp.

One fatal bite and he would be no more, but I only had a small taste to sustain my evil convictions. He yelled in a loud fright as he reached his final climax. I could feel the sweat of his body as he shoved me from his embrace. He jumped to his feet grabbing his clothes from the floor as he stumbled trying to escape to the door. He held his hand over his bloody neck as he screamed for help.

Smiling wickedly, I rubbed my tongue over my lips as I enjoyed the sensation of his blood. My naked frame felt warm and tremendously well pleased. I sprang to my feet before he could actually reach the doorway catching this man before he even knew I had him. I gripped his shoulder as I placed my hand over his eyes making him wilt to the floor in a comatose state. I hadn't any choice but to erase his memory, clear his mind of this situation. He was being entirely too loud with his panicking. Dragging his limp body back to the bed I gently placed his clothing back onto his figure. I quickly draped a robe over my bare skin and grabbed a warm towel from the bathroom. Cleaning his neck from any signs of blood, I decided to get my funds from his wallet placing it back into his pants pocket. I eased him in a sitting position snapping my fingers in front of his face. He awakened instantly. In a state of confusion he asked, "Who the hell are you? Why am I in this room?"

I kindly explained to him as I caressed his cheek with my fingers, "We had met in the little bar downstairs. We had drinks and you had one too many, so, I brought you to my room to help you sober up. We were supposed to have sex, but you passed out during our actual intercourse."

Shaking his head, confused, he never responded. He stood in bewilderment and made his exit.

So, you see, this is how I manage to stay fed and survive. Mostly, nightly, but some evenings, I seduce them right in the bar or in a corner, taking just enough blood to sustain myself. I crave the blood, yet I crave the pleasure more on some nights. Of course, there is times I have to wipe their entire memory of me leaving them in a zombie state. Some live, some die. It's very rare I actually murder anyone, but when the need arises, I haven't a choice. Some of my desirable victims can become violent or afraid and I cannot deal with such rudeness. You see, I never take their life in my hotel room, I only drain them enough to hypnotize their brain to do something fatal after they leave my presence.

The sexual pleasure, the ecstasy of the blood, and the joy of the game makes me feel powerful, invincible. I love to feel desired and wanted by my victims. I enjoy watching them struggle to get away from me once they see my true nature, yet I never reveal my fangs until I get my full orgasm from them. Do I only seduce the rich men? Of course not, I enjoy the financially stable ladies that seem lonely and power hungry in their stressful careers. The ones who work all the time never having any time for enjoyment. Those are the ones who I have to put out a strong effort to lure back to my dwelling. The challenge is mystifying to me.

One such instance was on a stormy night. The rain was brutally falling outside. The little bar was in a miserable state, yet there was a handful of people mingling about. As I rested my face in my hands, I overheard a woman ask the bartender for a weird drink. This female ordered a cranberry and vodka with a splash of bourbon on ice. This struck my curiosity. I wasn't in a hunger for blood since I had fed only hours ago on a fine gentleman that dwelt in the corner booth of the bar. This lady's blood stirred my senses. I knew right away from her mere demeanor that she was going to be tough. I had to have her; I had to taste her.

After this lady placed herself in a seat at the bar, just a few chairs from me, I watched her sip her drink as she put some papers on the counter in front of her. It appeared she was in some type of marketing or sales. She was fully focused on her work material, so, I decided to ease closer to her. Relocating in the leather chair right next to her, I ordered a red wine from the bartender, which was my usual order. Nonchalantly taking a sip of my wine, I quietly cleared my throat and said, "So, are you here on a business trip or just passing through?"

The woman looked at me as she graciously nodded her head and went back to sipping her drink while reading her paperwork. I knew right then that this was going to be slightly a tough one. This casual lady wasn't even remotely interested in my presence. Catching the bartender's attention, I ordered another of her strange drinks since I noticed she was almost finished with the one she had. This little gesture triggered her attention as she respectfully declined, saying, "Thank you, miss, but I think I'm finished drinking for the evening."

"Are you quite sure, my lady?" I returned with a seductive question as I shyly winked my eye at her. "I mean, it is a rainy, dreadful night and it's a perfect time to let loose from working. You seem like the type of person who overworks herself on a daily basis. Besides, everyone needs a 'good time' at least once in their life."

After pulling her long, blonde hair into a ponytail, the lady began gathering her papers and putting them into a briefcase. Stopping suddenly, she took a deep breath and exhaled. This determined woman looked straight at me as she rolled her eyes and accepting the drink. I smiled wickedly.

After several hours of drinking and conversating childishly about this lady's stressful career, I finally convinced this overworked woman to accompany me to my room. She was extremely intoxicated now, so, my seduction would be smooth like a breeze. Walking arm in arm, I had to carefully balance this female as we approached the elevators.

Inside the elevator I propped her against the mahogany wall as the steel doors closed. Blowing my breath toward the ceiling of this elevator near the corner, I fogged over the security camera. Pushing the button on the elevator panel, the mechanism halted between floors. Returning my focus to this drunken lady, I quickly leaned in for a kiss. She easily kissed me back as she pulled me closer to her body. She moaned as I slid my cold hand into her suit pants straight to her warm pussy.

Please understand, she was very drunk off too many cranberries and vodkas at this point, so, I do not think she knew who or what was happening to her, or where she even was. She was breathing heavily now as I thrust my fingers inside her. I had to control myself or I would devour this mortal much too quickly. Her blood smelled so inviting to my undead senses. I could vaguely feel her intense heat between her legs as I continued to breach her moist vagina. She stiffened in a heated passion as she moaned louder. We were intertwined as in a couple's embrace as she squeezed my shoulders pulling me closer against her breasts. My lips sucked and teased her neck as I held her in place against the wall. My fangs pierced her throat as she reached her overwhelming orgasm. Her blood was so bitter from so much alcohol, but I didn't care.

After draining her of her blood almost to the point of death, I realized I had simply gained my pleasure from this being without having her touch my body in any way. She slowly faded as her eyes closed tightly. Gently, I eased her to floor of the elevator as I cleaned the blood from her neck with my tongue. Removing my hand from her wet, forbidden area, I carefully situated this woman's attire in a proper fashion. With her limp body propped upon the wall, I felt her pulse in her wrist. There was still a heartbeat, but faintly. Deciding it best to leave her where she was, I placed my hand over her shut eyes and cleared all her memory of meeting me. Pushing the button on the elevator switchboard, I hit the number seven. I figured someone would mingle into this elevator eventually to find this poor mortal. If she survives, it would strictly be up to her.

I left this beautiful lady in the floor of the elevator as I made my way to my secluded room feeling full and completely satisfied. So, you see, this is how my lonely, undead life goes damn near on a nightly basis. I must admit, I enjoy the painful, yet amazing seduction, the misleading, the playfulness of the game, and the mystery of luring these mortals into my evil grasp. It's almost too easy sometimes. I've remained in this hotel for four years and never has anyone been suspicious of my seductions. I've relocated many times over the centuries, yet this place is definitely my favorite dwelling.

Everything seemed to be going great in the world of seducing these unaware mortals until one late evening when I saw him, Matthew. When I saw his narrow face glistening in the pale light of the barroom, a feeling shot through my entire undead body. This warm feeling was unlike anything I'd ever felt, but before I tell this part of my tale, I have one more 'lust' game I'd like to share...

On some nights, I find it is exciting, thrilling, to lure two, maybe three, mortals at a time back to my apartment. One such instance comes to mind that went considerably wrong. I was lingering, as usual, in the little hotel bar one late evening drinking my red wine as best I could at the end of the bar, when I noticed a small group of local college students mingle their way into the establishment. They were already strongly intoxicated and boldly asking the bartender for some whiskey shots. After consuming their shots, I watched them seat themselves at a corner table. Seemingly, several moments slipped by as a few of the students made their leave with only the two guys and one girl still sitting at the wooden table. They were flirting with each other in a sexy way as the girl with the long braids playfully kissed the guy with the wavy black hair.

Thinking to myself, "Should I join them and get in on the fun?"

Deciding I would try, I gracefully approached these loud adolescents, placing my glass of wine onto their table as I eased into the seat next to the guy with blonde curly hair. Looking concerned, the girl with the awful braids asked, "Who the hell are you? Why are you seating yourself at our table? This is a private function."

I could see the blonde male was very interested in my presence, but the selfish girl was skittish of me.

"Well, my lady, I'd like to join you in your fun, if I may. Should I buy a round of drinks?" I responded seductively.

"We can afford our own drinks, miss, but thanks anyway." The dark-haired male answered as he continued kissing the girl's neck.

I could tell this girl was a little bothered by my presence since it seemed as if she wanted these two guys for herself tonight. So, I hastily said, "No worries. I only wanted to partake in this playful seduction. I have a nice room on the seventh floor if you guys would like to move the party upstairs."

The strange girl quickly responded, "No thanks", telling me they were 'just leaving' as she grabbed the male's hand with the dark hair and motioning for the smiling, blonde male to follow her.

As they made their exit, I cautiously followed behind them. The challenge intrigued me, I suppose. Besides, I was not very fond of this smartass girl.

I noticed they were heading straight to Central Park as they stumbled over each other trying to keep their drunken balance. Watching as the girl leaned against an oak tree with the black-haired male teasingly seducing her, I realized that the other male was just sitting on the grass at their feet gazing at them with lustful eyes. I figured this was my chance! Quietly, I eased up to the blonde male, placing my arms around his waist as I lifted him from the ground. He freely gave in to my embrace as he kissed my cold, moist lips.

"I knew you wanted me." This blonde-haired mortal whispered as he continued to kiss my neck.

The two lovers against the tree gave no interest, only continued with their passionate lovemaking. As I began kissing this guy, I slowly caressed his dick in his thick jeans while he moaned in pure pleasure, all the while his dick getting extremely hard. Sucking on my neck, this male began touching and rubbing me as he tried to reach my forbidden vagina. He was trying to please me by caressing my heated area. I must admit, he was not very good at it. Finally, I had enough for tonight!

This just wasn't satisfying my own dark desires; besides, we were out in public, and it was much too acceptable to be noticed by someone. Deciding it best to end this boring seduction, I brutally yet quietly, drained this blonde-haired male of his blood dropping him to the dampened grass. Quickly, I gripped the dark-haired guy as I held tightly to the girl's throat against the tree. Sucking the blood from this male until he fell limp to the dirty ground. Turning my focus to the braided haired girl that I held in my grasp, I placed my hand over her eyes as she screamed in fear. I figured I would erase her memory while I sank my fangs into her warm flesh. When I felt this girl weaken in my arms, I dropped her to the grass next to her lover.

Leaving the three college students where they lay, I made my way back to the hotel. I'm not sure why I had to have those mortals, but at first, I was interested. Somewhere along the way, I lost that interest and decided to just have their blood instead of their pleasures. It seems the older mortals with better sexual experiences fulfill my lustful desire much better. The younger ones seem to be too bold and more aggressive in their seductions, much too demanding. Although, their blood was satisfying yet it was bitter from all the alcohol consumption they had partaken in.

I believe it was the challenge of these younger mortals that intrigued me. I just can't stand rejection! The disrespect of that braided-haired girl made me slightly furious. I haven't a clue rather those mortals lived or died. Part of me did not care. This experience was the only time I had trouble getting an orgy party together. Most of the time, it was quite a breeze to lure a group of older mortals back to my room to enjoy a lustful, romantic feast.

Now, I will tell my small tale of Matthew. The one male that gave me a great challenge to seduce him. Like I said earlier, I first saw him at the hotel bar that late evening and had a strange, warm sensation go throughout my undead body.

Part 2: The Courtship

I could see this mortal male was different from all the others I had seduced. I could sense his blood was strange, yet I knew he was a human. It intrigued me. I wanted to taste his blood and feel it spread throughout my undead body. I started feeling a strong yearning for this mysterious guy to touch my forbidden area with his masculine hands, to feel his lips kiss my breasts as he caressed my entire body. This sensation was about to madden me when I heard him order a beer from the bartender. Watching him for a short moment, I tried to study his muscular figure through his attire.

It appeared to my imaginations that his body frame was slightly toned and well-fit. Everything in me wanted to stroll my fingers and palms across his entire body. I wanted to slowly touch him, I wanted to taste him and his blood, and I wanted to place my lips onto his masculine domain. I assumed his dick was of a nice quality and size and would give the exact amount of lustful pleasure that my undead body needed. I wanted to feel his warmth upon my cold, chilled skin and feel his manhood enter my moist, throbbing vagina as he kissed my freezing lips with his heated passion.

Blinking my eyes a few times as if to snap out of this overheated seduction in my mind bringing me back to reality, I decided to casually make my way to the mahogany bar where this gorgeous male was seated. He was sipping on his cold beer as he stared off into space in deep thought. It was driving me crazy to know what he was thinking!

Ordering another glass of red wine, I cautiously asked this guy, "Why such deep thoughts?"

Turning his head to look at me, he only nodded with a crooked grin as he returned to his private gaze, tasting his alcoholic beverage. Rolling my eyes, it frustrated me! I wanted him to speak to me, at least, acknowledge my presence with a form of gratitude, but he was severely wrapped up in his own depressing mind!

After dwelling next to him in this leather bar chair for what felt like hours, I finally broke the silence and spoke to him again.

"I'm Veronica." I said boldly. "Who might you be? Are you from around here or just travelling through?"

Placing his beer bottle onto the bar, he answered in a determined tone as he looked right at me, "I'm Matthew, and my business is my own."

"Well, excuse me! I meant no rudeness to you, sir. I just wanted to make 'small' talk since you seem to be the only person in this secluded bar that offered an interesting type of conversation tonight."

"Understandable, Miss Veronica." He said sarcastically. "But I'd rather be alone, if you don't mind."

Catching the rude hint, I only smiled as I graciously took my glass of wine and made my way back to my usual little table in the darkened corner of the room. This was going to be tough, but I would not give up until I had this 'Matthew' before this night was over. I just needed to watch him a little longer, maybe try to figure out what intrigues this strange man. It maddened me yet engrossed my senses as to why this guy was not remotely interested in me. I was beautiful, sexy, and confident. So, why was this guy not falling into my seduction?

Confused, I stared straight at him. I knew he could feel my stare. Finally, he glances over at me, showing no expression as he returned to his private gaze while continuing to finish his second beer. Frustrated within myself at this point, I walked hastily, straight up to him placing my wine glass hard onto the wooden bar right next to him.

"I can see you are some kind of a 'loner', but there is no need to be so cruelly rude and ignore me."

Laughing a small chuckle, he replied, "Well, Miss Veronica, if you must know so badly, I'm on a dreadful business trip that I do not want to be on. My boss is a jerk, and it sucks! I had no choice but to come to New York only to rip off a small company and overtake their assets.

So, forgive me if I'm not in the mood to be seduced by a lovely lady on this night."

There it was. My chance to find out more about this strange man. Obviously, he was aggravated with his type of lively hood. Motioning for the bartender to bring another round of drinks, I seated myself next to him as I slid his beer in front of him. Accepting the beer, Matthew said, "Thanks for the beer."

"You're welcome." I smugly replied as I smiled. "Seems you could use one more."

"No shit." He said in return as he grinned back to me.

After several moments of awkward silence, I finally asked, "So, would you like to talk about it? I mean, I'm a complete stranger to you. I know nothing of who you are, so, I'd be a perfect candidate to hear your story."

"No, thanks. I'd rather drink my beer and try to forget my frustrations for now."

"I understand, I suppose."

Taking my hand, I gently started to play seductively with his hair on the back of his neck as I moved my body close to his.

"I could ease your mind if you allow me to. Make you forget about your frustrations for the rest of the evening." I whispered in his ear in a sexual, quiet tone as I leaned in to kiss his fragile lips, trying to seduce this man as best I could.

Slamming his beer bottle onto the bar, he stood quickly, pushing me away from him as he stated, "No thanks, but I appreciate the offer."

Unfortunately, I watched him walk away feeling maddened, rejected. This was honestly the first victim I ever lost. It frustrated me but I did not want to kill him just yet. He was too mysterious to rid him of his life at this point. Oh, how I hated rejection! Deciding I would secretly follow him, I noticed he went to the elevator getting off at the

5th floor of this hotel. So, that's when I returned to the bar to await a mortal of less interest. I would angrily devour a few mortals this night out of mere frustration. At least, I now know he's within this building, but for how long would be the important question.

I found myself dwelling, lingering, in the little bar over several nights without feasting or feeling any type of pleasures, all in hopes of this 'Matthew' coming back. I even walked to the 5th floor of the hotel on a few occasions trying to locate his room. No such luck! I felt like I was becoming obsessed, like a type of crazed stalker.

Finally, one late night, I was sitting in my normal spot in the corner of the bar still thinking about Matthew, when it happened. He walked into the bar and seated himself in the leather chair ordering a whiskey shot and a beer.

Part 3: Love or Lust?

That particular late night changed my immortal life, my viscous routine, for an eternity. I wasn't quite sure if it was actual love or just mere lust, but I knew this Matthew was not all that interested in me. It bothered me greatly. I hated to be rejected. I had to have him physically, mentally, and lustfully. Of course, it was a challenge but eventually I succeeded. I believe this actual challenge is what lured me to him. Was it just pure lust or was it actually love? Guess it will forever be a mystery. This is the tale of how I overtook my Matthew...

As I pondered on the idea of ripping Matthew's throat out as I watched him sip his beer at the bar across the room from me, I felt angered. How could he just reject my presence, my proposal, and my beauty? It was becoming personal now; I would have him. I didn't care if it meant killing him. He would be mine. I was determined at this point.

Deciding to make my presence known again to him this night, I slowly eased over seating myself at the bar just a few chairs from him.

I ordered something different than my usual drink, a bourbon on ice. I began gazing in his general direction as to be obvious. The bourbon was extremely sour to my taste, but it seemed to keep me calm.

As he continued to sip on his cold beer, I slowly eased my agitation. As I was about to speak in his direction, Matthew spoke first. He turned his head looking straight at me....

"Look, Miss Veronica, I want to be left alone." He stated boldly. "But, if you are so intent on seducing me, let's get it over with. Where is your room? Shall we go?"

He stood grinning a crooked smile toward me as he held out his hand in a gesture for me to get up. Laughing to myself, thinking this seems too easy, I graciously took his hand leading him toward the elevators. I felt I had won this challenge, yet I knew he didn't exactly want me. I understood it was only 'lust' for him, but I did not care. I would claim this victory!

Entering my room, I quickly embraced Matthew before he could change his mind, kissing him very passionately that it seemed to have shocked him. He began kissing me back, but with much more force. Our clothes began falling off as we fell onto the queen-size bed. Pressing his nicely toned body against mine, I stopped him, suggesting we first take a romantic bath in the little porcelain tub in the bathroom.

Rolling his eyes at me, he patiently waited for the warm water to fill the tub. His erection was so intense as he stood next to me against the counter. I slowly stepped into the bathtub turning the water off, seating myself in the refreshing water. I began caressing my breasts while he watched. Taunting him to join me in the water, he was reaching the point of explosion. Viciously, Matthew pulled me from the water carrying me back to the bed. He whispered in my ear, "Pleasuring oneself can be extremely seductive and fascinating!"

I could tell he was very much tempted and turned on. I had completed my job in luring him in. Tossing me onto the messed-up bed, he hastily placed himself on top of my wet, cold, naked body. His skin was extremely moist, hot, and sweaty. This aroused my senses. Reaching for the pillowcase next to my head, I ripped it off the pillow as I placed it around Matthew's eyes holding it tightly. I wanted to be more seductive, more playful, but he torturously ripped it from my grasp, saying, "No. I want to see all of you."

Looking at me as if he could see straight to my undying soul, he started to tease my nipples with his fingers. He whispered to me, "Your breasts are so porcelain-like, and your nipples are simply beautiful."

Before I could reply, he roughly began sucking my nipples and teasing them with his heated tongue. They were so hard and perky; it would've been too much pain for a mortal woman. Lust was coursing through my undead body; unlike any I've ever experienced. This mortal male knew how to arouse and pleasure a woman! Suddenly, I felt like my body would explode!

He placed his massive, hardened dick into my heated, wet vagina. I could feel his entire body tense up as he unloaded his manhood inside me. During this ecstasy, I totally forgot I was immortal and how much I wanted to taste his blood. Lying next to one another and feeling completely satisfied, I started to smell the scent of his blood, but my body was still in a type of limbo, ecstasy.

Matthew drifted into a deep sleep as I lay next to him just staring at his fragile face. He was such a beautiful man. It's a shame that I may have to feast on him very soon. The blood running through his vein was becoming so unbearable to my immortal senses. Right at the point where I was going to bite his neck, he woke up.

Stopping myself from piercing his vein, I only kissed him on his neck. He lifted my head placing his lips to mine. After a brief moment of sexual intimacy, Matthew stood and began placing his clothes back on, saying, "Let's get a drink at the bar now. I need a strong one."

Not responding to him, I followed his lead. Getting dressed; I accompanied him to the little bar downstairs. Ordering two bourbons on ice, we sat at the mahogany bar, neither of us speaking a word. Just gazing at this masculine man, I smiled. I was dwelling on how he had pleasured me only moments ago. No mortal has ever pleased me in this way! I pondered on why I haven't taken all his blood yet. Maybe, I felt funny, like a mortal lady that was falling in some type of love. Matthew stared straight in front of himself as I knew he felt my intense stare. It was obvious that he was pondering about our sexual encounter too. Before I could break the silence between us to ask about his thoughts, this petite woman from across the room yells "Matthew" as she walks right up to him, saying, "There you are. I've been looking for you for hours. Where have you been?"

Without answering her, Matthew takes this woman by the arm and rushes her to the elevators leaving me alone. I became furious! That rude bastard just left me here! No explanation as to why or who this bitch was! As a monster, I was severely angered! I knew I wasn't justified to be this angry within myself, but it still infuriated me! Even though, I'm a brutal fiend, I still felt as if I had been played a 'fool' by Matthew.

Finishing my strong iced beverage with its bitter taste irritating my tongue, I slammed the glass onto the bar countertop. Leaving the little bar area, I made my way to the elevators up to the 5th floor. I knocked on every hotel door on that floor until I found Matthew's room. Maybe I was being like a mortal, jealous girl, but I was angry.

When that same petite woman opened the door, I went into a heated rage. I grabbed her by her throat as I pushed my way into the hotel room. She never had a chance to scream as my fangs pierced her vein in her neck. This poor lady never knew what had her. I drained her to her death without a drop of blood left inside her lifeless body. At this point, Matthew ran from the steaming bathroom wrapped in a towel with his body dripping wet.

"What the hell have you done?" was all he could scream as he shoved me away from this pitiful woman. Trying his best to revive her, Matthew pleaded for me to call for help as he continued to curse me excessively.

Smiling devilishly, I never said a word in response to his pleadings. I only tasted the warm blood from the victim on my lips as I watched Matthew try his best to save his dead friend. Finally, he gave up on saving her. He jumped to his feet in anger and came toward me as if to harm me for taking this woman's life.

"You murdered my wife, Veronica! What the hell were you thinking?" Matthew shouted at me as he gripped my throat, squeezing hard with both his hands trying to stop my airflow.

He was brutally strong for a mortal male, if only he knew this was pointless, I could not die! Realizing that I was not human, he stumbles back in shock or fear when he noticed my sharp fangs that still had his wife's blood dripping from them. Terrified, he turns to run for the door that was still opened, but it was useless. I swiftly attacked him from behind sinking my teeth deep into his neck.

He was completely lifeless now, gone.

Gathering Matthew and his poor wife from the carpeted floor, I gently placed their dead bodies onto the king-size bed. Making my leave, I closed the door and never returned. I left them in their room on the 5th floor to be found by someone else.

Part 4: Only Eternity

The next evening, I packed my few belongings, checked out of the hotel, and left this beautiful residence in Manhattan. My time here was interesting and fun, but I hadn't a choice but to leave. Of course, I found myself feeling 'guilt' for Matthew and his poor spouse, but I am immortal, a monster, so the feeling doesn't linger for too long.

In my unjustified defense, I find that the humanistic reality was simply this...'The Vampire's Betrayal was more than Matthew could bare... Goodbye Matthew... It's over. It's done. It is finished, yet I feel I betrayed myself.'

Was it mere 'lust', the challenge of rejection, or could it have been 'love' that I felt for Matthew that night? I suppose it will forever be a mystery now.

I never said that my little tale was a romance. I wished it could've been, but sometimes 'love' or 'lust' can be deadly.

I now reside in London; my location and residence will remain unknown now. My memories of Manhattan and of Matthew only surface on rare occasions, yet I will always remember our intercourse of pure ecstasy. I try to forget the aftermath, but it creeps in at times.

I still feed on mortal victims who seem wealthy. I will play with such mortals in a reasonable routine on a nightly basis just as before, yet I made myself a promise to never again pursue an unwilling individual. It just isn't worth the 'guiltiness' I felt that night in New York. Rage and jealously is something I will not allow myself to ever feel again, definitely not 'love' or any type of sensual feelings for my victims from now on. I seduce, I feed, and I leave. I get my needed fill of blood and pleasure and move along.

Time fades away and it can't be stopped. One cannot change it.

I do believe now that I could've loved Matthew if it had lasted longer, and I did not act out in anger. Maybe that's why I couldn't drink his blood at first. He made me feel human again. The realization that he loved his wife was more than I could handle that night. Maybe it was just jealously on my part. Maybe it angered me to know he loved that petite woman, and I could never feel that kind of love.

Now I only have eternity to exist, as I set in this little sport pub on the outskirts of the city of London. I continue to watch these wretched mortals drink their drinks and try to hide their mixed-up emotions. I shall continue to prey on their blood and gain my personal pleasures. I shall never again let myself betray myself! I'm only existing in my eternity as an immortal beauty!

The Vampire's Betrayal

The End

$$\textbf{\textcolor{black}{—◆—}}$$

Short Tales Told
(Dark Stories of Love & Lust)

Also on Ebooks!

Available on Audiobook...
Sacred Choice (Between Good & Evil)
The Gothic Lady (Love Story)
Seductions of a Vampire
The Vampire's Betrayal

Short Tales Told
(Dark Stories of
Love & Lust)
By: Jo Ann Atcheson Gray, Jo Jo Gray,
Anna Elizabeth, & Sasha Joy

9 798330 337033